"I will turn the deserts into pools of water, and the parched ground into springs"—Isaiah 41:18b

An Urgent Appeal

To Christian Leaders in America for Consensus
and Collaboration on the Biblical Nature
and Hope of Corporate Revival

The National Revival Network

NAVPRESS

A *Pray!* Magazine Book
Pray! Books • P.O. Box 35004 • Colorado Springs, CO 80935
www.praymag.com

Pray! books are published by NavPress. NavPress is the publishing ministry of the Navigators, an international Christian organization whose mission is to reach, disciple, and equip people to know Christ and to make Him known through successive generations.

© 2003 by The National Revival Network

All Rights Reserved. No part of this publication may be reproduced in any form without written permission from *Pray!* P.O. Box 35004, Colorado Springs, CO 80935. Visit the *Pray!* website at www.praymag.com.

Unless otherwise identified, all Scripture quotations in this publication are taken from the *HOLY BIBLE: NEW INTERNATIONAL VERSION*® (NIV®). Copyright © 1973, 1978, 1984 by International Bible Society. Used by permission of Zondervan Publishing House. All rights reserved. Some quotations are from the *NEW KING JAMES VERSION* (NKJV), copyright © 1979, 1980, 1982, 1990, by Thomas Nelson Inc., Publishers.

Printed in the United States of America

1 2 3 4 5 6 7 8 9 10/ 07 06 05 04 03

Contents

Preface: A Nationwide Call 5

Introduction: The Appeal 7
America and Beyond
Starting the Conversation
The Title
Making It Personal

The Seasons of God 11
Judgment and Hope
Waterless Pits
Is There Hope

Definitions of Corporate Revival 15
Three Scholars Speak
Biblical Emphases
Terms and Metaphors
Cycles of Revival
Revival Is Christ!
Four Tests
A Suggested Pattern
Some Working Definitions

An Apologetic for Corporate Revival 23
The Decisive Person
The Divine Pattern
The Dark Prospects
The Disturbing Paralysis
The Dramatic Preparations
The Distinctive Praying
The Determined People

Three Key Clarifications 27
Sovereignty and Means
Point and Process
Repentance: A "Gift of Grace" and a "Divine Command"

A Series of Cautions 31
   Ignorance
   Shortsightedness
   Fantasies
   Superficiality
   Irresponsibility
   Negativity
   Uniformity
   Immaturity
   Elitism
   Nationalism
   Conflict

Responses to the Hope of Corporate Revival 35
   Perceive
   Prioritize
   Purify
   Pray
   Proclaim
   Prepare
   Partner

Appendix A: Some Questions and Answers 39

Appendix B: The Gospel of Jesus Christ—An Evangelical Celebration 45

Appendix C: Declaration of Intent 55

Teaching Curriculum for Facilitators .57

Preface:
A Nationwide Call

In San Francisco in January, 1998, nearly forty denominational leaders, on behalf of the 400 members of Mission America, signed a newly issued *Nationwide Call to Prayer to the Church in America*. Subsequently, *The Call* was published as a full-page ad in *USA TODAY*, signed by denominational leaders such as Bishop George McKinney (Church of God in Christ), Robert Watson (Salvation Army), Thomas Trask (Assembly of God), Robert Reccord (Southern Baptist Convention), William Hamil (Evangelical Free Church), and ministry leaders such as Billy Graham, John Perkins, Paul Cedar, Bill Bright, Jesse

> *"You will arise and have compassion on Zion, for it is time to show favor to her; the appointed time has come. . . . for the LORD will rebuild Zion and appear in His glory. He will respond to the prayer of the destitute; He will not despise their plea."*
> *—Ps. 102:13-17*

Miranda, Ron Sider, and more than 100 other national Christian leaders. Since then it has circulated widely throughout the body of Christ.

The Call has two parts: "A Call to Extraordinary Prayer" and "A Call to United Action." It sets forth consensus on an agenda for prayer and calls for collaboration in mobilizing concerted prayer. The focus of *The Call* is corporate revival. As such, it provides a major step toward the document you now hold.

This newer document, *An Urgent Appeal to Christian Leaders in America for Consensus and Collaboration on the Biblical Nature and Hope of Corporate Revival,* is designed to bring about even deeper levels of consensus and collaboration around the focus of *The Call* which reads in part:

> In recognition of our absolute dependence on God; The moral and spiritual challenges facing our nation; Our national need for repentance and divine intervention; Our great hope for a general awakening to the lordship of Christ, the unity of His body, and the sovereignty of His kingdom; The unique opportunity that the dawn of a new millennium presents to us for offering the gospel of Christ to everyone in our nation—

We strongly urge all churches and all Christians of America to unite in seeking the face of God through prayer and fasting, persistently asking our Father to send revival to the church and spiritual awakening to our nation, so that Christ's Great Commission might be fulfilled worldwide in our generation.

In the spirit of *The Call* and with its vision, the National Revival Network of Mission America has drafted, with input from nearly 100 national Christian leaders, *An Urgent Appeal.*

> —The Drafting Committee, *on behalf of*
> The Mission America Coalition,
> The National Revival Network,
> America's National Prayer Committee

The Appeal: An Introduction

America and Beyond

The primary audience of *An Urgent Appeal* is Christian leadership in America. However, the general principles are equally applicable to revival issues in the church worldwide. *The Appeal* celebrates significant renewal and revival movements in other parts of the world that illustrate many of the issues explored here. They hold out great hope for God's mercies to yet reawaken the church in America

Starting the Conversation

An Urgent Appeal is not intended to be a "primer" on revival. Instead, it presents an analysis on revival that attempts to be biblical, simple, and generally self-evident. The goal is to capsulate major themes on revival around which consensus and collaboration can be built as the American church stands at a new threshold in the kingdom purposes of Christ.

> "I keep asking that the God of our Lord Jesus Christ, the glorious Father, may give you the Spirit of wisdom and revelation, so that you may know him better. I pray also that the eyes of your heart may be enlightened in order that you may know the hope to which he has called you."
> —Eph. 1:17-18

The primary objectives of *The Appeal* include:

- **To cultivate** and promote increased consensus and collaboration about what the Holy Spirit has said and is saying concerning corporate, biblical revival.
- **To establish** a starting point for in-depth discussion on biblical revival by leaders of various denominational and ethnic backgrounds.
- **To provide** common language and a context within which Christian leaders can work together to foster this vision throughout the body of Christ.
- **To help** leaders who seek corporate, biblical revival to preempt unnecessary chaos and division among ourselves and our people as God grants our prayers for revival.

Ultimately, it is hoped *The Appeal* will stimulate collegiality among Christian leaders and will help cultivate a climate conducive to a theologically sound reawakening to Christ within our churches and throughout our nation.

The Title

A brief survey of its title may help further clarify the purpose of this document:

Urgent—We are standing at a crossroads moment in the life of the American church. Many believe we are at the threshold of a season of either revival or further judgment.

Appeal—This is an invitation to give immediate attention to the topic of revival. The document is consciously prophetic, calling Christian leaders to repent and wait on God with expectant hearts.

Christian Leaders—If a new work of God is on the horizon, the leaders must lead the way, and must do so together.

In America—This document addresses all North American Christian leaders, at all levels, in all parts of the body of Christ, across ethnic, denominational, generational, and ministerial boundaries. Further, it deals preeminently with the condition, needs, and hopes of the North American church. However, most of the document is relevant to Christians worldwide.

For Consensus—This *Appeal* does not require total agreement or total uniformity of thought. Instead, as one dictionary puts it:

> Consensus means: group solidarity in sentiment and belief; a general agreement; to give assent or approval; expression of common vision on which common action can be taken.

For Collaboration—Urgency requires more than intellectual assent. Leaders must also find ways to act together to meet the challenge of the hour. The dictionary defines collaboration as follows:

> To work jointly with others; to labor in and advocate for a common endeavor; to cooperate around fulfilling a shared mission.

Biblical—This *Appeal* is to Christian leaders who see the Scriptures as the final authority and ultimate measure of truth on the subject of revival. The more theological precision we can gain, the better we can navigate together between revival and "revivalism."

Hope—This refers to any God-given vision for the future that is shaped by the Christ-centered promises of the Scriptures.

Corporate—Revival deals with the affairs of Christ's church. In Scripture it is preeminently a corporate phenomenon. Thus, this document speaks primarily to corporate revival. At the same time, it recognizes that community-wide renewal will always include the reviving of individuals.

Revival—Fuller definitions will be found in the following pages. To this end, the rest of the document will:

- Provide a brief analysis of our need for revival.
- Give definitions to the hope of biblical revival.
- Set forth an apologetic for confessing such a hope in our generation.
- Survey three major affirmations about revival.
- Identify important cautions.
- Propose practical responses leaders can make together.

Making It Personal

Finally, please note that at the conclusion of each section there are a few application questions and other exercises designed to help the reader (whether alone or in a small group) to engage *The Appeal* on a personal level. These sections will also assist readers in determining further steps they might take toward consensus and collaboration. This document was drafted with one special group in mind, the local ministerial fellowship or pastoral prayer group. Each section of *An Urgent Appeal* provides content for discussion and prayer, using the "Reader's Reflections." All of this could be developed into a sermon series on the biblical nature and hope of corporate revival.

The Seasons of God

Judgment and Hope

One year passes into another, one century into another, one millennium into another. Great leaders, great movements, great nations come and go. Only a few things remain. Only a few things stand the test of time.

God's truth remains, as His Word will not pass away. When God speaks, it is sealed in heaven—sure, dependable, alive.

There are clear patterns in Scripture regarding how God speaks. Sometimes He speaks messages of warning. Sometimes He speaks messages of hope. With His Word come seasons . . . epochs of His special activities, across the centuries, in fulfillment of His Word.

> "As for you, because of the blood of my covenant with you, I will free your prisoners from the waterless pit. Return to your fortress, O prisoners of hope; even now I announce that I will restore twice as much to you."
> —Zech. 9:11-12

For those who do not heed the warnings, there come seasons of judgment. For those who do heed and repent, the Holy Spirit gives seasons of new beginnings—resurrections, as it were.

Yes, God does judge—both individuals and whole civilizations. Sometimes His judgment is remedial. His discipline is meant to bring a people to their senses, to lead them to turn and to return to Him.

At such crossroads moments, God ultimately confronts His people with their sin. They have grieved Him deeply by embracing the idols of their age. Offended by their betrayal, He turns away. He must uphold the honor of His holy name among the nations. He withdraws the showers of His blessing (Ez. 34:26). The rains of His righteousness are withheld (Hos. 10:12). His people find themselves in "waterless pits" (as He terms them in Zech. 9:11). Yet, the God of everlasting love, the "God of hope" (Rom. 15:13) is not far from His covenant people. He continues to call them to pray, to repent, to turn from their idolatry and unbelief, and to once again place their wholehearted trust in Him alone. Then He summons them to hope. To seasons of renewal, restoration, revitalization, reformation . . . *revival.*

Waterless Pits

What does God see as He looks at the North American church?
Many claim that the church in America may be the most organized, populous, financially prosperous, visible, and culturally pervasive of any Christian movement in the history of the world. Reports of renewal abound: liturgical, theological, ecumenical, charismatic, lay, youth, missionary. Volunteerism and faith-based ministries remain strong. Stadiums overflow with zealous disciples. There is much for which we can praise God.

But what else does God see in the church? Despite the glitz and glamour, does He also find waterless pits? Is there a sense that in spite of all our measurable activity, the church generally is paralyzed? Are we outwardly prosperous while being inwardly weak and stagnant?

Do the great doctrines of the Bible fail to grip our congregations and move the hearts and minds of our people? Does religious flesh and fleshly religion dominate, marked by self-sufficiency and self-promotion? Have we so domesticated Christ and privatized the gospel that we have become impotent in our impact on the social and spiritual crises of our nation? Is this why there has been negligible overall church growth nationwide during the past decade? Many church leaders would sadly confess it is so.

Research tells us that there is little difference between the lifestyle of Christians inside the church and our society as a whole. The disintegration in our culture is also found in our churches: racism; hypocrisy; hero worship; materialism; busyness; lack of social conscience; road rage; disintegration of the family; pornography; abortion; status quo mediocrity; self-indulgence in our abundance; self-satisfied with our kingdom accomplishments. The sad part in all of this is that the living Christ Himself is marginalized; He is not glorified as the Supreme Lord of the church.

What does God see as He looks across America?
Surely God sees spiritual erosion, moral bankruptcy, and the loss of fixed, transcendent values and absolutes. Mother Theresa concluded that America's "poverty of the spirit" was the greatest poverty she found anywhere. Traditional American religious impulses may be up, but morality and ethical cohesion are down, unchecked by a flourishing neo-paganism that has become the serious pursuit of multitudes of our citizens.

In addition, God sees our 50 million urban poor, where a gap between rich and poor grows wider every year. He knows that half our marriages end in divorce. He grieves that we have lost our sense of the sanctity of life, that we have become increasingly a culture of death. He beholds the incarceration of millions of our citizens. He sees our self-consuming consumerism. All of it: "waterless pits."

Christians today, like Israel before them, find themselves wandering in a desert of their own making because they have too often chosen what was expedient and disobeyed God. Many have become "nominal Christians," possessing a form of godliness but forfeiting the power of God.

In this condition, we must pause and face a sober and humbling truth: The hope of revival is not offered to the Church Militant but rather to the Church Repentant. There is a danger here. If the church is blind to its true spiritual condition, then revival will simply be viewed as a divine additive, given basically to increase the effectiveness of our ministries instead of restoring the glory of God in His church.

But once we recognize how far we have fallen (Rev. 2:4-5) and again realize our covenant relationship and responsibilities to God, then we will humble ourselves, pray, seek His face, turning from our wicked ways. It is then we learn the ancient yet ever relevant lesson that the road to revival is paved with contrite and broken hearts. With such a people our God is pleased to dwell (Is. 57:15). Repentance is the pathway to revival.

Is There Hope?

In the extended hands of a forgiving God comes the offer of hope (Hos. 14:1-4). Our waterless pits can become pools of living water as the refreshing rains of His Spirit return to pour upon us again (Hos. 6:1-3).

Our God is a God of *promises*. His promises focus on new beginnings, seasons of renewal, especially for those in waterless pits. The Holy Spirit desires to take us together where we have never gone before, just as He has done with His people so many times in the past.

He is able, for He remains forever the God of revival. Should we not speak of it and prepare for it with full resolve, and without any reserve? Can we not trust Him in this? Since to the whole church the Holy Spirit proclaims, Christ is in you, the hope of all the glorious things to come (Col. 1:27), how can we trust Him for less?

As you look at the landscape, what do you sense? Are we at a threshold? Is it too late? Or is there a season of hope before us? Is it a time to get ready for an extraordinary awakening to Christ—to get ready for biblical revival? Do you sense an urgency?

Nationally respected Christian leaders have expressed hope for a comprehensive work of God's renewing grace among American Christians in this crucial hour. It is an extraordinary hope, a claim that, despite our sin and paralysis, God desires to do something radically new with His people. It is an expectation of an amazing work within Christ's church in our nation that actively engages us in the power of the Holy Spirit to transform our cities and culture, to evangelize our friends, to touch unreached peoples worldwide. *Revival!*

An Urgent Appeal is presented by the National Revival Network of Mission America in the conviction that multiplied Christian leaders across America increasingly desire to pursue consensus and collaboration for corporate revival, and to help their people to do the same.

MAKING IT PERSONAL: READER'S REFLECTIONS

- What are some of the developments in the moral and spiritual condition of the United States at this present time? Do you think that the essay you just read was accurate in describing these factors? Or, did it go too far? Why or why not?
- Do you feel the essay was too hard or too soft on the condition of the church of Jesus Christ in the United States? Why do you feel this way?
- The essay says: "Nationally respected Christian leaders have expressed hope for a comprehensive work of God's renewing grace among Christians." On what might such a hope be built? Are you hopeful? Why or why not?
- Where can I/we find common ground with other leaders in the issues covered within this section?
- Centered on Christ, do I/we have sufficient consensus about the previous section to proceed to explore the next section together?
- Is there a prayer response that would be appropriate right now before I/we move to the next section? (Spend time praying.)
- Scripture for meditation: Is. 49:5-20; Acts 11:19-25.

Definitions of Corporate Revival

Three Scholars Speak

Let's call on three evangelical scholars, with well over 100 years of scholarship and five earned Ph.D.'s between them in the study of biblical and historical revival. They provide us with excellent definitions as a starting point for our considerations.

First, J. Edwin Orr distilled his decades of research into the following definition:

> *An Evangelical Awakening is a movement of the Holy Spirit* bringing about a revival of New Testament Christianity in the church of Christ and in its related community. Such an awakening may change in a significant way an individual; or it may affect a larger group of believers; or it may move a congregation or the churches in the city or district, or the body of believers throughout a country or continent; or indeed the larger body of believers throughout the world. The outpouring of the Spirit affects the reviving of the church, the awakening of the masses, and the movement of uninstructed peoples toward the Christian faith; the revived Church, by many or by few, is moved to engage in evangelism, in teaching, and in social action.

Theologian J. I. Packer concurs with this perspective when he writes:

> Revival, I define, as a work of God by His Spirit through His Word bringing the spiritually dead to living faith in Christ and renewing the inner life of Christians who have grown slack and sleepy. In revival God makes old things new, giving new power to law and gospel and new spiritual awareness to those whose hearts and

---

"This is what was spoken by the prophet Joel: 'In the last days, God says, I will pour out my Spirit on all people.' . . . 'The promise is for you and your children and for all who are far off—for all whom the Lord our God will call.' . . . Repent, then, and turn to God, so that your sins may be wiped out, that times of refreshing may come from the Lord."
—Acts 2:16-17,39; 3:19

consciousness have been blind, hard and cold. Revival thus animates or reanimates churches and Christian groups to make a spiritual and moral impact on communities. It comprises an initial reviving, followed by a maintained state of revivedness for as long as the visitation lasts.

Writing as a senior pastor, and former Old Testament professor, Raymond C. Ortlund Jr. provides a vivid description of revival:

> When God rends the heavens and comes down on His people, a divine power achieves what human effort at its best fails to do. God's people thirst for the ministry of the Word and receive it with tender meltings of soul. The grip of the enslaving sin is broken. Reconciliation between believers is sought and granted. Spiritual things, rather than material things, capture people's hearts. A defensive, timid church is transformed into a confident army. Believers joyfully suffer for their Lord. They treasure usefulness to God over career advancement. Communion with God is avidly enjoyed. Churches and Christian organizations reform their policies and procedures. People who had always been indifferent to the gospel now inquire anxiously. And this type of spiritual movement draws in not just the isolated straggler here and there but large numbers of people. A wave of divine grace washes over the church and spill onto the world. That is what happens when God comes.

Biblical Emphases

Revival, by whatever term, appears to be a distinctive and recurring pattern in God's work with His people. Church historian Dr. Richard Lovelace observes that God's predisposition is always toward revival: "The great theme of Scripture is God's recovery of an apostate people." Yale scholar Kenneth Scott Latourette, in his seven-volume work on Christian history, observed that there were "ebbs and flows" of the Christian movement over the past 2,000 years that invariably issued out of seasons of spiritual awakenings.

More importantly, the Bible itself contains revival narratives, revival prayers, revival predictions, and revival principles. Thousands of verses deal with the promises of God for revival, the ways of God in revival, the manifestations of God during revival, the impact of God on His people out of revival, the personal and corporate dimensions of revival, and, ultimately, the centrality of Christ throughout any revival. Although the theme is set forth under both the Old and New Covenants, in the latter there is a much greater range of God's work in revival because it is now secured, mediated, and expanded through the finished work of the ascended Christ.

From one perspective, revival is where all the purposes of God ultimately end up. The last two chapters of the book of Revelation describe what some have called the "Final Revival," of which every other season of revival is a prototype. Every historic revival is, in a sense, an "approximation of the Consummation"—that is, an intermediate expression, or a preliminary but substantial demonstration, of Christ's kingdom in all of its glory. It is a dress rehearsal, if you will, of the climactic "renewal of all things" that transforms heaven and earth when Jesus returns.

Terms and Metaphors

That being said, in time and space and history, revival comes according to patterns generally revealed throughout the Scriptures and church history. As a result, a number of terms have emerged to delineate various facets of biblical revival. These include:

- Renewal
- Awakenings
- Effusions of the Spirit

- Fillings of the Spirit
- Quickenings
- Restorations
- Christ-awakenings
- The manifest presence of Christ

- Reformations
- Visitations
- Outpourings of the Spirit

- Baptisms of the Spirit
- Revitalizations
- Times of Refreshing
- Jubilees

Various metaphors have also been used such as:

- Waking up
- Fire falling
- Deserts blossoming like a rose
- Winds of renewal
- Overthrowing of the status quo
- Seasons of springtime and harvest

- Latter rains
- Turning back captivity
- Rivers of renewal
- Beneficent sabotage
- Spiritual revolution

Whatever the term or metaphor, most would agree that revival is a season when God mercifully turns away His judgments from the church, deserved because of her lukewarmness and disobedience. Instead, God moves to comfort and restore her, to intensify, accelerate, deepen, and extend the work of His Son in and through her.

Cycles of Revival

Latourette's metaphor describes revival epochs as waves of the sea washing up the shore as the tide comes in. Implied in that picture is the fact that there are episodes of advance and recession throughout the history of God's people—cycles, some call them.

This is not to suggest some kind of arbitrary interpretation that causes previous awakenings to limit or predetermine our expectations of the steps God might take in some future outpouring of the Holy Spirit. We can never put God into some kind of a "revival box."

Yet seasons do unfold, and patterns can be seen. Why have cycles of revival been required through the ages?

Again, our consideration is with corporate revival rather than personal revival. Most agree it is possible for an individual believer to live in continuous renewal, or "revivedness" (Packer), even if the Christian community around him is in spiritual recession. But regarding corporate revival, there are at least five reasons for the cycles or waves:

1. **Spiritual gaps,** as a new generation rises up that does not know Christ in the depth and intensity of former ones.

2. **Previous blessings,** which have, over time, fostered a sense of self-satisfaction and complacency in the body of Christ.

3. **Theological neglect,** that has permitted imbalances and divergences that diminish or obscure our vision of who Christ really is as well as our theological precision.

4. **A new era of expansion,** when the re-awakening of the church is related primarily not to God's rescuing her from judgments, but to God's intention to reactivate the church for new advances of the gospel in our communities, throughout a nation, and among the unreached peoples of the world.

5. **God's sovereignty.** Sometimes there is no other apparent explanation except that God chooses to do so for the glory of His Son simply because He is God.

Revival Is Christ!

Preeminently, all true revival is about God bringing glory back to His Son by the power of the Holy Spirit through His church. Between the Ascension and the Consummation, this is one of the most strategic activities of the Holy Spirit. In fact, corporate revival necessitates Trinitarian activity: Father-initiated, Spirit-driven, Son-centered.

Yes, biblical revival is supremely Son-centered—it is utterly Christ-dominated. Some have even called it a "Christ-awakening." We can only think rightly about revival when we think rightly about Christ's place in revival. He is the criterion by which we define it, measure its legitimacy, and vindicate its impact.

This is the heart of the consensus we seek. Further, our collaborations must coalesce around Christ. Any spiritual experience, whether called revival or something else, that diminishes Christ, bypasses Him, or actually leads away from Him, is not of God and holds no hope for any generation.

> *The first issue before us as Christian leaders, then, is not to define the characteristics of revival. Rather, it is to comprehend more fully the Christ who is at the center of corporate revival.*

Fundamentally, revival is an awakening to all that Christ already is for us. Saint Irenaeus said: "Christ brought us every newness by bringing us Himself." In the same way, in revival God does not make new things. Rather, He makes things new. He does this by reintroducing us to Christ who stands at the epicenter of His renewing purpose among the nations. As said earlier, in revival God accelerates, intensifies, deepens, and extends the newness that Christ secured for us. Revival increases our capacity to express this newness and to minister it to others. In revival God invites the church into more of who Christ is for us, even as we invite Christ into more of who we are for Him.

After all, Scripture's revival promises were secured for us by the cross of Christ. The cross marks the most decisive moment in God's ongoing commitment to "the recovery of a backslidden people." Everything that revival brings has been bought and paid for by the blood of Jesus. In addition, the message of the cross exposes, rebukes, and replaces every false hope on which the church might depend, giving us the greater hope of God's inexhaustible and unconditional renewing grace. The cross acts as a hinge to open the floodgates of God's reviving bounty for any generation of His people.

Four Tests

Four Christological tests of the legitimacy of anything calling itself "revival" might be applied:

Existential—God's people? Does it give evidences of His lordship over peoples, institutions, and the powers of darkness? Does the Holy Spirit have greater freedom to manifest the ministries of Christ among His people?

Ethical—Does it multiply evidences of Christ-likeness throughout congregational life? For some, does it increase a spirit of daily repentance or efforts at racial or denominational reconciliation?

Ecclesiastical—Does it sharpen and empower the life and work of a local congregation in such things as worship, teaching the Word, prayer, spiritual gifts, love for one another, and outreach with the gospel?

Eschatological—Does it appear to be, in principle, a reflection of the final revival; that is, an approximation of the consummation? Does it reinvigorate the church to work toward the end by spreading the gospel in ministries of social reform, compassion to the poor, justice, reconciliation, community transformation, as well as the many facets of global missions?

A Suggested Pattern

In conclusion, whether revival is chronologically near or not, we can be certain the Holy Spirit always keeps it Christologically near. To use another term, revival is about arrival—when, through the Spirit, Christ shows up afresh (as it were) to invade His church, to capture and conquer us anew, to re-energize us with His eternal purposes, and to take us with Him to fulfill them more fully than ever. No wonder the 18th century New England Puritans called corporate revival, quite simply, "the manifest presence of Christ."

As noted above, a general pattern in biblical revival, observable throughout church history, highlights this dominance of Christ in all revival. The pattern might be outlined in this manner:

- **Realization:** Revival desired. A people alerted to seek more of Christ.
- **Preparation:** Revival sought. A people repentant and ready to receive more of Christ.

- **Manifestation:** Revival received. A people confronted and changed by more of Christ.
- **Consecration:** Revival applied. A people devoted to live more for Christ.
- **Revitalization:** Revival absorbed. A people enlivened to express more of Christ in all of life.
- **Penetration:** Revival unleashed. A people actively sharing more of Christ by word and by deed.
- **Expansion:** Revival fulfilled. A people taking more of Christ to the nations.

Some Working Definitions

Revival is utterly Christological. Along with the views of Orr, Packer, and Ortlund above, other working definitions that capture this might include:

"Revival is the church falling in love with Jesus all over again."
(Vance Havner)

"Revival is a community saturated with God." (Duncan Campbell)

"A revival means days of heaven upon earth."
(D. Martyn Lloyd-Jones)

"Revival is ultimately Christ Himself, seen, felt, heard, living, active, moving in and through His body on earth."
(Stephen Olford)

"Revival is God purifying His church." (Erwin Lutzer)

"Revival is that strange and sovereign work of God in which He visits His own people, restoring, re-animating, and releasing them into the fullness of His blessings." (Robert Coleman)

"Revival is a sudden bestowment of a spirit of worship upon God's people." (A. W. Tozer)

"A true revival means nothing less than a revolution, casting out the spirit of worldliness and selfishness, and making God and His love triumph in the heart and life." (Andrew Murray)

"Revival is the reformation of the church for action."
(Max Warren)

"Revival is God revealing Himself to man in awful holiness and irresistible power. It is God's method to counteract spiritual decline and to create spiritual momentum in order that His redemptive purposes might be accomplished on earth"
(Arthur Wallis)

Whatever definitions we create, those who have lived in a season of revival record three consistent, Christ-honoring dimensions: (1) In revival God gives His people a renewed focus on Christ's person. As a result, (2) we experience together in new ways the fullness of Christ's life within the church. (3) All of this presses us into new involvements in the fulfillment of Christ's mission, both where we live and among the nations.

Whatever definition one may favor, it appears that in the end, revival is Christ!

MAKING IT PERSONAL: READER'S REFLECTIONS

- In your circle of relationships, is the term "revival" understood the way it is set forth in this section? Why or why not?
- What definition of revival resonates best with you? Why?
- Do you agree with the reasons given for "cycles of corporate revival?" Why or why not?
- Are there any other tests that you would add to the four given in this section regarding the validity of a revival?
- Where can I/we find common ground with other leaders in the issues covered within this section?
- Centered on Christ, can I/we find sufficient consensus about the previous section as I/we proceed to explore the next section together?
- Is there a prayer response that would be appropriate right now before I/we move to the next section? (Spend time praying.)
- Scripture for meditation: 2 Chron. 15:1-7; 1 Jn. 4:1-7.

An Apologetic for Corporate Revival

Christian leaders will seek consensus and collaboration on corporate revival to the degree they are thoroughly convinced it is a legitimate, necessary expectation for their generation. Without such confidence, we will be reluctant to invest in something that simply may never happen.

In 1 Pet. 3:15 we are told to be ready at all times to give an answer to those who demand reasons for the hope that is in us. Often, however, Christian leaders struggle to maintain confidence about the hope of revival, and thus to lead their people into the same vision. This happens for a number of reasons, including:

> "The people were waiting expectantly and were all wondering in their hearts . . . John answered them all: . . . 'He will baptize you with the Holy Spirit and with fire. . . . [He will] gather the wheat into his barn, but he will burn up the chaff with unquenchable fire.' And with many other words John exhorted the people and preached the good news to them."
> —Lk. 3:15-18

- **Lack of study** on the ways of God in corporate revival.
- **Ignorance of the cycles** or seasons of revival throughout church history.
- **Insipid rationalism** that causes us to function, for all practical purposes, as if the supernatural is of little consequence.
- **A sense of being overwhelmed** by the great needs of the body of Christ and the mission of Christ in our generation, as we face difficulties and challenges that seem almost insurmountable.
- **Personal disappointments** from past ministries that make it difficult to trust God for a greater work today in the life of the church at large.
- **Weariness** in the midst of current personal ministries that inhibit one's ability to reflect on the larger work of God in revival.
- **Isolation** from other leaders who have this hope and who promote it among their people.

Thankfully, there are multiple reasons to embrace and foster the hope of corporate revival with confidence. For leaders who are growing in their desire to see revival, the following seven-fold apologetic is offered. It is not intended to take the place of the hundreds of biblical promises for revival. This apologetic is supplemental—a unique way to organize the rationale for our hope. It can buttress our consensus and galvanize our labors. At the same time, these seven arguments can double as fresh perspectives on all that corporate biblical revival encompasses.

The seven-fold apologetic includes:
1. The decisive person
2. The divine pattern
3. The dark prospects
4. The disturbing paralysis
5. The dramatic preparations
6. The distinctive praying
7. The determined people

The Decisive Person

The Scriptures promise repeatedly that God intends for His Son to be decisively at the center of everything, both at the end of history and every step along the way. In revival, God dramatically intervenes to restore a vision for, and increased responses to, Christ's rightful role as redeemer King among His people; and to more fully advance His kingdom, right now, among the nations. Therefore, because of God's ultimate commitment to His Son "to bring everything out at His feet for disposal" (E. Stanley Jones), we can pray and prepare for corporate revival with confidence that our hope is not in vain.

The Divine Pattern

God is faithful and consistent in all His ways. He has been pleased to grant seasons of significant revival both in biblical times and in church history. As Scripture teaches, He is no respecter of persons. What He has done before, in other times and places, He is able and willing to do for our generation. The specifics may vary, but the patterns have been documented. And the promises in both Old and New Testaments are pervasive. Therefore, because of God's commitment to His own time-honored procedures for glorifying His Son, we can pray and prepare for corporate revival with confidence that God will not disappoint us.

The Dark Prospects
God loves the world and longs to see His Son exalted among all earth's peoples. But He knows the world is currently facing extraordinary crises and challenges beyond its own resources. Furthermore, nearly three billion of earth's peoples are still outside the reach of the gospel. Revival in the church can uniquely transform the church and make her equal to the desperate needs of our times. It is a supreme hope, held out to us throughout Scripture, for a greater harvest in the world He loves. Therefore, because of His commitment to the mission of His Son on behalf of the nations, we must pray and prepare for corporate revival.

The Disturbing Paralysis
God knows that the desperate condition of the world today is due, in large measure, to the state of the church. He sees our struggles with powerlessness, brokenness, dullness, carnality, and sin. Yet, the Bible clearly teaches that God intends to bring glory to Himself through the church, not apart from it. The church, however, cannot heal her own impotency and paralysis. The shining hope for this to happen today is for God to restore us powerfully as a people, by His grace. This healing of an invalid church is called revival. Therefore, because of God's commitment to the body of Christ, we can pray and prepare for revival with confidence that He will not forsake His many promises to grant it.

The Dramatic Preparations
The tools God has provided and the doors He has opened for fulfilling the Great Commission today form nothing less than the prelude to corporate revival. God is obviously setting the stage worldwide for a whole new advance of Christ's kingdom among millions of unbelievers. Since these multiplied preparations of resources and laborers and renewal movements are His sovereign design, He will not fail to fulfill what He has begun. Therefore, because of God's commitment to bring to completion every good work raised up in and for His Son (Phil. 1:6), we can seek revival according to God's promises.

The Distinctive Praying
In unprecedented fashion, God is stirring up His people everywhere to pray biblically, specifically, increasingly, and persistently for local, national, and even worldwide revival. Beyond question, God never calls His people to pray in vain. His Word promises that He will hear, and answer fully, prayers instigated by His Spirit. Therefore, because of His commitment to respond proactively toward all prayers made according

to His will—prayers that come from, through and for His Son—we should prepare eagerly and confidently for the answer: corporate revival.

The Determined People

God is galvanizing a host of people across our nation (and worldwide), convinced by the undeniable promises of His Word that revival is a dynamic hope for the church and for Christ's kingdom to advance among the nations. In addition, they are willing to pay any price to prepare the way for God to grant it. Not only are they a chief sign of the "impendingness" of an awakening to Christ, they are actually the first phase of it. They are the Spirit's gift to the church for this strategic hour.

Therefore, because of God's commitment to vindicate ultimately the servants of His Son who pray and prepare for corporate revival, we can rest in confident hope.

This seven-fold apologetic relates not only to a sweeping massive revival, which may be in the offing; it also encourages us to live expectantly about revival right where we live—in our own lives, and churches, and regions.

Asking It Personal: Reader's Reflections

- Which of the reasons listed (page 23) for why Christian leaders often lose confidence about the hope of revival do you identify with most?
- Are there specific steps you might take to confront any of these barriers in your life?
- Of the seven-fold apologetic for revival, which arguments do you personally find most compelling and why?
- Can you identify anyone in your circle of relationships that you could say is one of the "determined people." If so, what are some ways that you might unite with them to encourage each other to pray and prepare for revival?
- Where can I/we find common ground with other leaders in the issues covered within this section?
- Centered on Christ, can I/we find sufficient consensus about the previous section as I/we proceed to explore the next section together?
- Is there a prayer response that would be appropriate right now before I/we move to the next section? (Spend time praying.)
- Scripture for meditation: Hos. 6:1-3; Is. 57:14-15

Three Key Clarifications

In keeping with the title of Jonathan Edwards' 1748 publication on prayer and revival, our *Appeal* for consensus and collaboration is equally, "an humble attempt to promote explicit agreement and visible union of all of God's people" in the hope of a corporate awakening to Christ.

> *"LORD, I have heard of your fame; I stand in awe of your deeds, O LORD. Renew them in our day, in our time make them known; in wrath remember mercy."*
> —Hab. 3:2

Consequently, it is important to face up to some of the critical issues over which the church has deliberated for generations in defining the essence of biblical revival. In this section, the main issues of controversy have been condensed into three "clarifications." In the next section, we will look at eleven "cautions" related to these issues that need to be considered. Discussing them can help foster a common meeting ground for Christian leaders on the issue of revival. The three clarifications are:

- Sovereignty and Means
- Point and Process
- Repentance: A "Gift of Grace" and a "Divine Command"

Sovereignty and Means

Most would agree that ultimately no work of Christ is ever accomplished by human means. It is not by might, but by the Spirit of the Lord (Zech. 4:6). God is sovereign in corporate revival. In the final analysis, human beings cannot predict its timing, precipitate its unfolding, nor preclude its appearance. None of us can extort it from God by human methods or activities, however earnest we may be.

Corporate revival comes from God alone, beyond our resources, ingenuity, or control. No human-designed formula can compel God to grant it. The church cannot plan it, stage it, or organize it. It is not ours to create; it is ours to receive. No church committee or team of revival specialists can engineer it. It may be church-obtained, but it is Christ-attained. This is the distinguishing mark between revival and a human-produced "revivalism."

However, the "Primary Agent" of revival (the Holy Spirit) can and does make providential use of secondary means. Often He chooses to work in grace through our prayers, Bible studies, worship, fellowship, sacraments, and daily obedience. There may be nothing Christians can do to guarantee corporate revival at any particular moment. But we can always intensify our preparations for God's gift, in keeping with our faith and hope in His promises.

In other words, biblically speaking, intervention calls for preparation; sovereignty encourages advocacy. God promising to be the producer of revival motivates us with expectation of revival among fellow believers. We might say: "Consecrate yourselves, for tomorrow the LORD will do amazing things among you" (Josh. 3:5). Or like Isaiah: "give [God] no rest till he establishes Jerusalem and makes her the praise of the earth" (Is. 62:7). Or like Jesus: "The time has come, . . . The kingdom of God is near. Repent and believe the good news" (Mk. 1:15).

Point and Process

Corporate revival is both a point in time as well as an ongoing process and experience in the life of the church. Frequently in Scripture, as well as recorded in church history, the motif of dramatic encounter and visitation—the rending of the heavens, the pouring out of the Spirit—is used to describe the uniqueness of revival as a point in time. (Review other terms and metaphors listed earlier.) In this sense, corporate revival is seen as extraordinary, radical, the resurrection of a people exhausted, diseased, and sick with sin.

But the decisive moment of the Spirit's reclamation of a people leads to an ongoing process of increased fruitfulness and impact in the church's life. This may last a generation or more.

In other words, a greater intimacy with Christ leads to a stronger walk of obedience to Him. Poignant, extraordinary displays of grace will bring sustained infusions of grace into ordinary disciplines of the church. The qualitative nature of a church-wide revival has quantitative implications that are normally long-lasting. Authentic inward transformations translate into measurable outward demonstrations of the ministry of Christ through His people.

Without God's quickening intervention (point), all of our efforts at reformation or unity (process) will ultimately turn sour or simply wither away. However, God's visitations (point) reaffirm sound doctrine, renovate church structure, and encourage the body of Christ to stand together in the cause of Christ (process). Revival not only supplies what is absent (point) but then multiplies what has been unleashed (process). Reviving (point) results in revivedness (process).

In fact, corporate revival need not simply fill a vacuum. In some cases it serves to quicken, intensify, enlarge, and fulfill the very best elements of current renewing activities of the Holy Spirit already underway. Accordingly, it would then reactivate spiritual gifts, encourage existing community transformations, compel emerging racial reconciliation, motivate further social reformations, and re-ignite ongoing personal evangelism and missionary endeavors.

In either case, as the church is awakened to the person, presence, and power of Jesus Christ, the society around it will be spiritually aroused, possibly resulting in a long-term "general awakening" as we have seen at least three times in our own national journey (i.e., the First, Second, and Third Great Awakenings).

Repentance: a "Gift of Grace" and a "Divine Command"

Repentance presupposes grace (Acts 11:18). For individuals deserving of God's judgment because of sin, the possibility for repentance is itself based on God's kindness and patience. Thus, repentance is a gift from God, a means for sinful people to experience restored relationship with God based on the atoning work of Christ.

Yet, repentance is also a divine command to the church (Acts 17:30). Christ commands earnest repentance while He "knocks," rebuking His people for illusions of self-sufficiency and lukewarmness. Although this kind of brokenness is painful, our position in Christ as believers frees us to face our sinful condition and to mourn over the ways we grieve His Spirit. With broken hearts turning from sin, we are enabled to turn to Christ for times of refreshing (Acts 3:19).

Other questions for clarification are incorporated into "Appendix A." You may want to glance at it before going on to the "Reader's Reflections."

Making It Personal: Reader's Reflections

- Why is it important for us to embrace both sovereignty and means? What are the pitfalls of neglecting God's sovereignty? What are the pitfalls of neglecting the means?
- How does the knowledge that corporate revivals have a starting point encourage you? What are your favorite terms to describe such divine moments? Can you share about one you have experienced or read about?
- Are there dangers in being too point-centered? Too process-centered?
- What would it mean for leaders to unite locally in the revival process in a way that prepares us for a wonderfully surprising revival point?
- Are there other questions for clarification that you would like to explore in the Appendix?
- Where can I/we find common ground with other leaders in the issues covered within this section?
- Centered on Christ, can I/we find sufficient consensus about the previous section as I/we proceed to explore the next section together?
- Is there a prayer response that would be appropriate right now before I/we move to the next section? (Spend time praying.)
- Scripture for meditation: Ex. 14:10-18; Phil. 2:12-13; 2 Tim. 4:2; Jas. 5:7-11; Acts 3:19-20.

A Series of Cautions

Although the biblical hope of corporate revival foresees extraordinary blessings in Christ (as outlined in this document), there are also serious cautions we must heed, even dangers at certain points. It is best to recognize and clarify them now, to be ready to confront them if and when they surface.

Some of the cautions include:

> "Then suddenly the Lord you are seeking will come to his temple; . . . But who can endure the day of his coming? Who can stand when he appears? . . . He will purify the Levites and refine them like gold and silver."
> —Mal. 3:1-3

Ignorance
A general misapprehension of how God deals with His people in revival, due to our neglect of biblical and historical study of the topic; or due to our blindness to where and how God is currently granting seasons of renewal and awakening within the church. This could create a temporary climate of confusion, chaos, and division in fostering the message of revival, or during an awakening itself.

Shortsightedness
Limited views of the term revival—such as it being an evangelistic campaign, the restoration of individual backsliders, the refreshing of a local congregation, or a duplication of the outward forms of a previous general awakening. This could lead us to a parochial hope that settles for less than God's best for our generation.

Fantasies
Expecting God to do more than He actually has promised regarding corporate revival. This might lead us to seek manifestations of revival that have no clear biblical warrant, or to spread reports on revival that exaggerate what really happened. Our hope must be in harmony with what God has said and not our own wishful notions. Similarly, it is unhealthy to expect current outworkings of corporate revival to mimic the specific characteristics of some previous revival for another generation. Disappointment is likely.

Superficiality
The temptation to seek revival rather than to seek God; to seek phenomena rather than to seek His presence. The Scriptures and the Spirit always work together. Sound doctrine will always accompany true revival, helping Christians to engage more fully the manifest presence of Christ as the heart of revival. The revival movement cannot be allowed to become primarily testimonial or story-fed, rather than Bible-fed and God-centered.

Irresponsibility
Seeing revival as a panacea, a magic wand encouraging us to excuse ourselves from responsible obedience and follow-through in the day-to-day struggles of the church, whether God grants revival or not. Our seeking revival must be accompanied by daily obedience — whether in love, or worship, or outreach, or ministry to the poor — even as we live in anticipation of more to come. We must do what God has clearly told us to do, even while we pray and prepare for what God has promised He will do.

Negativity
Overlooking all the ways God is blessing now; failing to affirm the positive aspects of current kingdom advances; lacking gratitude to God for how many efforts of the church in our generation have effectively challenged and transformed the culture. Above all, we must avoid the tendency to depreciate current, normal, regular ministries of the Holy Spirit measurable, to some degree, in any believing Christian congregation.

Uniformity
Failure to appreciate the balance between continuity and diversity. The danger of division rests in our attempts to gain uniformity in a season of revival without reckoning with this fact: the outward shape of a reviving work is often based on prior conditions within each community experiencing it. These would include: pre-existing needs, the cultural context, ecclesiastical traditions, the age or temperament of those being revived, their previous spiritual experiences, their collective theological grids, and the extent of their current spiritual malaise. Even though there are common themes in every God-given revival — the centrality of Christ, confession of sin, quickening of the Scriptures, increased love, outreach to the lost — still, diversity of experiences must be expected and not be resisted.

Immaturity

A lack of preparedness for the exuberance, eagerness, excitement, and fresh expectations that normally come in seasons of revival. As was true with the awakening in New Testament Corinth, extraordinary experiences of God's power and presence run the risk of creating temporary disorder due to immaturity or carnal mismanagement of newly unleashed spiritual gifts. But a far greater danger is that fear of misplaced enthusiasms will drive people to settle for something worse (in the words of J. I. Packer): "the predictability, unexpecting apathy and tidy inertia of a congregation locked in spiritual deadness."

Elitism

Unconsciously justifying attitudes of arrogance or sectarianism on the part of those claiming to be revived. They perceive themselves to be a select group with special favors from God, spiritually superior to those not experiencing the same phenomena, or emotions, or breakthroughs, or reformations. This is another place where consensus and collaboration on revival among Christian leaders before revival comes can pre-empt a deadly trend. Guarding our unity must always walk hand in hand with the reformation of sound doctrine and the revitalization of spiritual life.

Nationalism

Expecting revival to salvage and rescue a whole nation when, in fact, it is a work of God promised exclusively for the people of God. Only secondarily does it impact a surrounding community, and only at times does God-given revival spill over to transform a whole culture or nation (sometimes termed a general awakening). Our motivation must not rise from nationalistic passions, therefore, but from our desire for God to get the greatest glory through His church—even if the nation as a whole rejects this gracious hope and undergoes subsequent divine retributions (as happened with Jerusalem in AD 70 despite a revived church in its midst).

Conflict

Entering into the euphoria and wonders of corporate revival without reckoning with increased levels of warfare with the powers of darkness or with persecution due to the impact of revival on unbelievers. Awakening often brings seasons of conflict and suffering. Out of reformation and revival, the church is drawn more fully into the vortex of Christ's mission among the nations. By manifesting more of

Christ to and through the church, revival arouses the antiforces—both human and spiritual—against Christ's kingdom. Revival sends the church actively into battlefields and harvest fields as we confront, contest, and displace the works of darkness. Suffering is therefore unavoidable and must be expected.

Conclusion

Are these cautions permanent obstacles to consensus and collaboration? Quite the contrary. Actually, sincere discussion by Christian leaders can significantly foster the common ground that will help prepare us to fully embrace together corporate, biblical revival as God grants it.

MAKING IT PERSONAL: READER'S REFLECTIONS

- The introductory paragraph reads, "It is best to recognize and clarify [cautions] to be ready to confront them if and when they surface." What difference could this make? Why?
- Can you think of any other cautions, either from the Word of God or from your own experiences, that should be brought up?
- In Mal. 3:1, a work of God is described as beginning "suddenly." What would be your response to a sudden move of God next Sunday, let's say, in your worship service? How do you think others in your church would respond?
- Where can I/we find common ground with other leaders in the issues covered within this section?
- Centered on Christ, can I/we find sufficient consensus about the previous section as I/we proceed to explore the next section together?
- Is there a prayer response that would be appropriate right now before I/we move to the next section? (Spend time praying.)
- Scripture for meditation: Acts 19:1-20; 2 Thess. 3:1 with 1 Thess. 1:1-10.

Responses to the Hope of Corporate Revival

A recent video on revival, *Hope for a New Millennium,* featured fifteen respected leaders speaking to the hope of revival for our nation. It concluded by calling the viewer to "Fear not! Spare not! Prepare for amazing things about to happen, maybe tomorrow— and do so with full resolve and without any reserve. Prepare with total abandonment because you can trust Christ."

It went on to challenge Christians to drive a stake in the ground. It suggests we say: "From this moment on, I sense the urgency. I am ready to embrace the hope that God sets before us. I will act as if I really believe that God will awaken His church afresh to Christ and His kingdom. I will get ready for corporate revival. And I will call others to join me."

This response means reconstituting our daily walk both with Christ and with fellow Christian leaders so that everything we do is compatible with our hope of renewal. It means getting back to the cross, getting clean before Christ, being broken before God, repenting of everything that entangles us. As leaders, whatever we sense God needs to do to salvage our churches and ministries, we must be willing for Him to do within our own lives first . . . no matter what the cost. We must "consecrate ourselves" (Josh. 3:5). Consensus and collaboration for corporate revival will come no other way.

Fundamentally, this means recommitting ourselves not simply to do more but to seek more. As we look out over the wasteland of our culture and of the American church today, we might be tempted to ask, "Do we have a prayer?" The answer, in one sense, is: "Yes. In fact, all we have is a prayer!" In other words, prayer is the most strategic response any of us can give to our needs for an extraordinary move of God in corporate revival. As Isaiah puts it: "You who call on the LORD,

> *"I counsel you to buy from me gold refined in the fire, so you can become rich; and white clothes to wear, so you can cover your shameful nakedness; and salve to put on your eyes, so you can see. Those whom I love I rebuke and discipline. So be earnest, and repent. Here I am! I stand at the door and knock. . . . He who has an ear, let him hear what the Spirit says to the churches."*
> —Rev. 3:18-22

give yourselves no rest, and give [God] no rest . . ." (Is. 62:6-7). Yet, our prayers must not stand alone.

The breadth of our response to this vision, particularly on a corporate level, might best be expressed a number of ways (including prayer). These are not sequential steps. Rather, they are dimensions of ongoing preparations (and even collaborations) for corporate revival:

Perceive—The first phase of every spiritual awakening comes as God's Spirit awakens believers to acknowledge not only that revival is urgently needed but that the promise of revival is for them. Subsequently, such heaven-given perception quickens the rest of our obedience.

Prioritize—Next, we must be willing to say: "A primary hope for my generation is revival in the church. Therefore, out of my commitment to the preeminence of Christ, I will give revival high priority. With a sense of urgency I will pray and labor to that end, in every facet of my role as a Christian leader."

Purify—In our own lives, as well as those we lead, repentance must have precedence. Everything that grieves the Holy Spirit—every sin, activity, or relationship that is incompatible with revival; every hindrance or obstacle to revival—must be confessed to God and put away. Holiness should become a shared passion. As long as we fail to repent of that which quenches, resists, or disobeys the Spirit, revival—which is preeminently an extraordinary work of the Spirit—will not be receivable. Repentance has always been a hallmark of a generation that experiences a corporate Christ-awakening. Corporate repentance, therefore, remains an evidence of a church moving toward godliness, preparing together for revival.

Pray—The time has come for spiritual leaders to fully embrace the unprecedented prayer movement raised up by God already in many churches and communities across our nation—to strengthen it and become much more active leaders in it. The "Nationwide Call to Prayer to the Church in America" (see Preface) goes on to recommend a four-fold National Prayer Accord that encourages unified revival praying on daily, weekly, quarterly, and annual bases.

Proclaim—Since "faith comes from hearing" (Rom. 10:17), any biblical revival must be a Word-anchored revival. Therefore, as leaders, we must become "messengers of hope" to the body of Christ. We must promote the biblical promises for corporate revival (of which there are hundreds of passages); give reports of what God has done in the past and is doing today in revival around the world; and help God's people envision what a revival in our generation might look like, both inside and outside the church. This message must be a predominant theme wherever and however we minister the Word of God.

Prepare—Though biblical revival is preeminently a corporate experience, individually each one of us must be willing and ready to become the starting point for a fresh work of God in His church. Personally and collectively, we need to live out a discipleship that is anticipatory. We should "act as if" we expect God to grant us this work of His Spirit. Our obedience to a significant degree should equip and prepare us for greater manifestations of Christ in the future. This outlook will impact our discipleship programs, our worship, our social endeavors, and our labors toward theological precision, as well as ministry partnerships among spiritual leaders.

Partner—We have now come full circle in a document that appeals for "consensus and collaboration." The hope of impending revival requires a new era of spiritual leadership—whether among local pastors, leaders of prayer movements, urban missionaries, denominational leaders, or others. The primary initiative, of course, should come from leaders of local churches in a given community. But there also needs to be—and increasingly are—national networks and coalitions holding forth this high priority, sharing their consensus across traditions, generations, and ethnicities. Currently, such coalitions include Mission America, Christian Community Development Association, America's National Prayer Committee, National Association of Evangelicals, National Revival Network, Denominational Prayer Leaders Network, National Pastors Prayer Initiative, National Network of Youth Ministries, National Association of Local Church Prayer Leaders, National Religious Broadcasters, and others.

In Conclusion

In the end, all the above responses represent different ways to heed Christ's revival call to the church in Laodicea (Rev. 3:20-21). Basically, the Spirit said to them: "Open wide the doors to Christ." As Christian leaders we must earnestly heed this call in our day.

Open wide! To Christ! Together! Freely! In hope! Let's get ready for His manifest presence. Let's welcome God's gracious gift of a fresh Christ-awakening for our generation.

To that end, let us continue, under Christ, to pursue consensus and collaboration. It will take nothing less to bring the church to the threshold of personal, local, regional, and even national revival. And such joint action must be sustained in order to shepherd the church during the seasons of corporate revival that, by God's grace, surely are not far off.

To join your name with others who are committing themselves to be about revival, prayerfully review the "Declaration of Intent," then go to www.urgentappeal.net and sign the document (or you can mail in the card attached to this booklet).

If you have questions regarding *An Urgent Appeal,* please refer to the question and answer form found on the following website: www.urgentappeal.net.

MAKING IT PERSONAL: READER'S REFLECTIONS

- Has the case been made for the "hope of corporate revival"? If yes, what is the most persuasive concept or idea for you? If not, what could be done to strengthen the argument so as to reassure you?
- Have you personally "driven a stake" on your own that has helped the preparation for corporate revival? If so, how have you expressed this? If not, why not? What is your next step?
- What changes would you need to make in your life and ministry if this hope of corporate revival were to become more dominant in your life and ministry?
- Of the seven ongoing preparations suggested, which is currently strongest in your life? Which is weakest? How would you answer the same questions for your home church?
- Where can I/we find common ground with other leaders in the issues covered within this section?
- Centered on Christ, can I/we find sufficient consensus about the previous section to move forward together? Is there sufficient consensus on the whole *Appeal* document to lay a foundation for collaboration? If so, where should we begin? Is there a prayer response that would be appropriate right now?
- Scripture for meditation: 2 Chron. 30:6-27; Acts 15:4-35; Heb. 10:23-25.

Appendix A: Some Questions and Answers

1. Is corporate revival really necessary?
If by "necessary" you mean that Christians cannot obey God, preach the gospel, pray, and make disciples as our Lord commanded, the answer is a resounding no! The church has clearly known blessing and help without revival. But revivals are still desirable and should be prayed for by the church because they display the glory of the gospel with the greatest effects to the watching world. Revivals are not God's only means of advancing the church, but they are a wonderful means of blessing that should be desired by His people—especially when they have endured long periods of drought and lifelessness.

> *It is important to consider several important questions that flow out of* An Urgent Appeal. *These are typical of the questions that repeatedly surface when the subject of revival is presented.*

2. If corporate revival does not come, should the church despair?
Not at all. How can those who know and love Christ as their Lord ever despair? We should recognize that judgment may well affect much of what is being done by the church in our time, yet we must still rejoice that "our names are written in the book." Even sorrow and chastisement can be mixed with joy through the filling of the Spirit. It must be understood that revival is never a panacea for the church. It is, however, a sovereign interruption that brings health and greater blessing to the work of the church.

3. If God is the sole author of corporate revival, then what is the point in becoming informed and exercised about this subject?
To say that we do not cause God to bless us is not to say that God does not bless us through biblically ordained means that must be used to accomplish His sovereign purpose. It is an unshakable truth taught throughout Scripture that we are utterly dependent upon God for all life, both physical and spiritual. However, we are never to passively wait for God to bless us, but rather we ought to pursue His blessings in complete dependence upon Him as the author and giver of every

good and perfect gift (see Jas. 1:17). Because He is such a great and awesome God, nothing is "too hard for the LORD" (Gen. 18:14). Our times are desperate, the hour is late, judgment clearly hangs over us, but no obstacle is too great for God.

4. Where is the Holy Spirit when there is no revival?

Jonathan Edwards might well have been the greatest theologian of true revival in church history. He wrote: "Though there be a more constant influence of the Spirit attending His ordinances, yet the way in which the greatest things have been done has been by remarkable effusions, at special seasons of mercy." Does the present prolonged delay of "remarkable effusions" indicate that the Holy Spirit has ceased to work? Are we at a significant disadvantage when revival tides are out? Our answer has a great bearing on how we live during those times when true revivals are scarce.

We are best served by understanding several basic truths revealed in Scripture about the present ministry of the Holy Spirit. We have the promise of Christ that the Spirit indwells His disciples (Jn. 14:16,26; 15:26; 16:7). Our Lord refers to the Spirit as "the helper," a word that emphasizes the Spirit's direct role in encouraging, helping, and counseling. The Holy Spirit assures believers that they are the children of God (Rom. 8:14-16) and that God loves them (Rom. 5:5). He also assures them that Jesus indwells their lives with His presence (1 Jn. 4:13) and that God's power is at work in them (Gal. 3:5). He makes Christ known to believers experientially (1 Cor. 2:10-12) and assures them of final victory in Christ on the last day (2 Cor. 5:5; Rom. 8:11,15-17,23).

Further, believers have peace given by the Holy Spirit (Rom. 14:17; see Jn. 14:15-19). This "peace" is a divinely given sense of well-being and contentment in all circumstances. The Holy Spirit floods believers' minds with the truth of God (Eph. 1:17-18) and convicts them of their need to change and grow in the grace of God (Rom. 8:5-9). He also gives believers gifts for spiritual ministry (1 Cor. 12:4-6; Rom. 12:6-8).

The absence of "remarkable effusions" does not mean that any of these ministries of the Holy Spirit are hindered in any way. As important as it is to pray for true revival, believers must never lose sight of this simple fact—God is actively working in every believer and in the church whether or not He grants wide-scale awakening. Believers should give thanks for the Spirit's powerful present ministry while continuing to ask that God "rend the heavens and come down" (Is. 64:1) in a remarkable season of revival.

5. But what part do we actually have in corporate revival?
Divine freedom never negates human responsibility. We can and must act in obedience to God. The mystery of the seeming tension between divine freedom and human responsibility must not be solved by rational syllogisms and logical inferences. We must obey as if everything depended upon them and pray knowing that the results depend upon God. Therefore, the first place to start in seeking God for revival is by removing all personal hindrances to real revival. Our personal sins grieve the Spirit (Eph. 4:30) and our collective sin quenches His work among us (1 Thess. 5:19). God is not pleased with our sins, and we must confess them and forsake them. If deadness and lack of real blessing characterize our assemblies, we have need to come to grips with the fact that the reason lies within us (Psalm 32).

We must also pray. We have biblical examples as well as biblical and historical precedent for such prayer. The divine commandment of God to His people is to pray. Both personally and corporately, believers should plead with God to reveal lukewarmness of their condition (Rev. 3:16).

Who of us can read Revelation 2 and 3 and not conclude that our Lord is speaking these penetrating words to the contemporary church? Who would not agree that it is we who "have forsaken [our] first love" (2:4) and we who "have a reputation of being alive, but . . . are dead" (3:1). The counsel of Jesus to the lukewarm congregation in Revelation 3 is: "I counsel you to buy from me gold refined in the fire, so you can become rich; and white clothes to wear, so you can cover your shameful nakedness; and salve to put on your eyes, so you can see" (3:18).

If we would spend time getting a true picture of our need—"wretched, pitiful, poor, blind and naked" (3:17)—we would run to Christ and ask Him to enter the door of our church afresh (3:20). The picture of Christ outside the church is a haunting image of a present reality.

6. Can I experience personal revival even if God is not pleased to send a great revival to multitudes?
There is no reason whatsoever for any believer to remain in sin or to live a life of frustration and spiritual deadness. At the same time, suggesting that there are formulas that, if followed, will inevitably bring revival is a prescription for massive failure and profound frustration. The believer should always confess sin, seek after God with the whole

heart, pray for the empowering of the Holy Spirit, and implicitly trust Christ every day. As we draw near to God, He has promised to draw near to us. However, to put demands upon God regarding how He must bless or use our lives is unbiblical.

7. Does our understanding of the future and of the coming of Christ have anything to do with the urgency of our concern for revival?

Christians have agreed on the essential elements regarding the biblical doctrine of the end times for 2,000 years—for example, that Christ will personally return at the end of this present age, that the resurrection will take place at this coming, that the judgment will follow, and that heaven or hell will be the ultimate destiny of every person who has ever lived.

At the same time, there have also been areas of disagreement regarding some of the details related to the scenario of the end. The three major debated views are known as premillenialism, amillenialism, and postmillenialism. There are still Christians who hold each position today, and each interpretation has experienced a period of ascendancy during different eras of church history, especially in America. While it is important to note that no major historic confession of faith or creed of the Christian church has ever made these debated points a test for genuine orthodoxy, it is clear that these views have exercised a major influence upon the church's interest in revival over the last three centuries.

Premillenialists view the Apocalypse in a future sense and believe that the events described in Revelation are yet to happen. However, prophecies of darkening world conditions do not preclude expecting revivals from God. In times like ours, when spiritual declension threatens to slow world evangelism, revival can still be seen in the Premillenialist system as an aid to complete the mandate given to the church to "go into all the world and preach the good news" (Mk. 16:15).

Amillenialists view the present church age as the fulfillment of the millennial period referred to in Revelation 20. They also take a number of the prophecies which futurists limit to Israel and apply them to the church. In this system, revival could simply be seen as a greater manifestation of the Holy Spirit's ongoing kingdom work.

Postmillenial thought differs from the other two major views in that it asserts that Christ's return will follow the period of "millenial blessing." Often this view has been satirized by those who accuse postmillennialists of believing that "things will get better and better until Christ returns." However, postmillennialists hold a strong hope for revival, not because they believe that world conditions will progressively improve, but rather because they believe world conditions do not have a determinative role in what a sovereign God might be pleased to do in revival at any point in human history. The darker the moment the more glorious might be the light of reformation and revival. Thus, this system can easily accommodate the idea of revival and apostasy running side by side until the day of the Lord.

One does not need to adopt any one of the above schools of prophetic interpretation to believe that "hope" for a great revival is actually grounded in Scripture itself. The vast majority of biblical commentators believe that no one view of prophecy necessarily precludes the possibility of real revival, either locally or internationally. Prophetic views need never diminish calls to prayer and hope for revival.

8. What is the nature of spiritual warfare during corporate revival?
The invasion of the Holy Spirit into a corporate body of believers in revival is nothing less than an all-out assault of the kingdom of God upon the forces of the kingdom of darkness. These demonic forces may be manifested through various Satanic strongholds, deceptions, and hindrances established in the hearts and minds of God's people through their disobedience, unbelief, and compromised allegiance to Christ.

We are told by John the Apostle that "the reason the Son of God appeared was to destroy the devil's works" (1 Jn. 3:8). This is no less true than when the Spirit of Jesus (Acts 16:7) is poured out upon His people in revival and upon the unregenerate in a spiritual awakening. Therefore, revival is a true power encounter. There is a collision of kingdoms where captives are liberated and new recruits are called forth from death and bondage to serve and give homage to Christ the King (Acts 26:18; Col. 1:13).

Our prime responsibility during these times of heightened spiritual combat in revival is not to develop an undue focus and fascination with our enemy and his counterfeits, but to thoroughly know the true characteristics and qualities of a genuine work of the Spirit of God. It is here, in the midst of the heightened activity of the Spirit of God, that the sword of the Spirit, the Word of God, is our most effective weapon (Eph. 6:17). In any war there will be wounds and casualties. But, we can reduce the damage in the next great revival battle by preparing ourselves, like the apostle Paul, in the art of kingdom warfare "in order that Satan might not outwit us. For we are not unaware of his schemes" (2 Cor. 2:11).

Appendix B: The Gospel of Jesus Christ
An Evangelical Celebration

Preamble

The gospel of Jesus Christ is news, good news: the best and most important news that any human being ever hears.

This gospel declares the only way to know God in peace, love, and joy is through the reconciling death of Jesus Christ the risen Lord.

This gospel is the central message of the Holy Scriptures, and is the true key to understanding them.

This gospel identifies Jesus Christ, the Messiah of Israel, as the Son of God and God the Son, the second Person of the Holy Trinity, whose incarnation, ministry, death, resurrection, and ascension fulfilled the Father's saving will. His death for sins and His resurrection from the dead were promised beforehand by the prophets and attested by eyewitnesses. In God's own time and in God's own way, Jesus Christ shall return as glorious Lord and Judge of all (1 Thess. 4:13-18; Mt. 25:31,32). He is now giving the Holy Spirit from the Father to all those who are truly His. The three Persons of the Trinity thus combine in the work of saving sinners.

This gospel sets forth Jesus Christ as the living Savior, Master, Life, and Hope of all who put their trust in Him. It tells us that the eternal destiny of all people depends on whether they are savingly related to Jesus Christ.

This gospel is the only gospel: there is no other; and to change its substance is to pervert and indeed destroy it.

This gospel is so simple that small children can understand it, and it is so profound that studies by the wisest theologians will never exhaust its riches.

> For God so loved the world that he gave his one and only Son, that whoever believes in him shall not perish but have eternal life.
> —Jn. 3:16
>
> Sing to the Lord, for he has done glorious things; let this be known to all the world.
> —Is. 12:5

All Christians are called to unity in love and unity in truth. As Evangelicals who derive our very name from the gospel, we celebrate this great good news of God's saving work in Jesus Christ as the true bond of Christian unity, whether among organized churches and denominations or in the many trans-denominational cooperative enterprises of Christians together.

The Bible declares that all who truly trust in Christ and His gospel are sons and daughters of God through grace, and hence are our brothers and sisters in Christ.

All who are justified experience reconciliation with the Father, full remission of sins, transition from the kingdom of darkness to the kingdom of light, the reality of being a new creature in Christ, and the fellowship of the Holy Spirit. They enjoy access to the Father with all the peace and joy that this brings.

The gospel requires of all believers worship, which means constant praise and giving of thanks to God, submission to all that He has revealed in His written word, prayerful dependence on Him, and vigilance lest His truth be even inadvertently compromised or obscured.

To share the joy and hope of this gospel is a supreme privilege. It is also an abiding obligation, for the Great Commission of Jesus Christ still stands: proclaim the gospel everywhere, He said, teaching, baptizing, and making disciples.

By embracing the following declaration we affirm our commitment to this task, and with it our allegiance to Christ Himself, to the gospel itself, and to each other as fellow Evangelical believers.

The Gospel

This gospel of Jesus Christ which God sets forth in the infallible Scriptures combines Jesus' own declaration of the present reality of the kingdom of God with the apostles' account of the person, place, and work of Christ, and how sinful humans benefit from it. The Patristic Rule of Faith, the historic Creeds, the Reformation confessions, and the doctrinal bases of later evangelical bodies, all witness to the substance of this biblical message.

The heart of the gospel is that our holy, loving Creator, confronted with human hostility and rebellion, has chosen in His own freedom and faithfulness to become our holy, loving Redeemer and Restorer. The Father has sent the Son to be the Savior of the world (1 Jn. 4:14): it is through His one and only Son that God's one and only plan of salvation is implemented. So Peter announced:

"Salvation is found in no one else, for there is no other name under heaven given to men by which we must be saved" (Acts 4:12). And Christ Himself taught: "I am the way and the truth and the life. No one comes to the Father except through me" (Jn. 14:6).

Through the gospel we learn that we human beings, who were made for fellowship with God, are by nature—that is, "in Adam" (1 Cor. 15:22)—dead in sin, unresponsive to and separated from our Maker. We are constantly twisting His truth, breaking His law, belittling His goals and standards, and offending His holiness by our unholiness, so that we truly are "without hope and without God in the world" (Eph. 3:12; see also Rom. 1:18-32, 3:9-20; Eph. 2:1-3). Yet God in grace took the initiative to reconcile us to Himself through the sinless life and vicarious death of His beloved Son (Eph. 2:4-10; Rom. 3:21-24).

The Father sent the Son to free us from the dominion of sin and Satan, and to make us God's children and friends. Jesus paid our penalty in our place on His cross, satisfying the retributive demands of divine justice by shedding His blood in sacrifice and so making possible justification for all who trust in Him (Rom. 3:25-26). The Bible describes this mighty substitutionary transaction as the achieving of ransom, reconciliation, redemption, propitiation, and conquest of evil powers (Mt. 20:28; 2 Cor. 5:18-21; Rom. 3:23-25; Jn. 12:31; Col. 2:15). It secures for us a restored relationship with God that brings pardon and peace, acceptance and access, and adoption into God's family (Col. 1:20, 2:13-14; Rom. 5:1-2; Gal. 4:4-7; 1 Pet. 3:18). The faith in God and in Christ to which the gospel calls us is a trustful outgoing of our hearts to lay hold of these promised and proffered benefits.

This gospel further proclaims the bodily resurrection, ascension, and enthronement of Jesus as evidence of the efficacy of His once-for-all sacrifice for us, of the reality of His present personal ministry to us, and of the certainty of His future return to glorify us (1 Cor.15; Heb. 1:1-4, 2:1-18, 4:14-16, 7:1-10:25). In the life of faith as the gospel presents it, believers are united with their risen Lord, communing with Him, and looking to Him in repentance and hope for empowering through the Holy Spirit, so that henceforth they may not sin but serve Him truly.

God's justification of those who trust Him, according to the gospel, is a decisive transition, here and now, from a state of condemnation and wrath because of their sins to one of acceptance and favor by virtue of Jesus' flawless obedience culminating in His voluntary sin-bearing death. God "justifies the wicked" (Rom. 4:5) (ungodly) by imputing (reckoning, crediting, counting, accounting) righteousness to them and ceasing to count their sins against them (Rom. 4:1-8). Sinners receive through faith in Christ alone "the gift of righteousness" (Rom. 5:17, 1:17; Phil. 3:9) and thus become "the righteousness of God" in Him who was made sin for them (2 Cor. 5:21).

As our sins were reckoned to Christ, so Christ's righteousness is reckoned to us. This is justification by the imputation of Christ's righteousness. All we bring to the transaction is our need of it. Our faith in the God who bestows it, the Father, the Son, and the Holy Spirit, is itself the fruit of God's grace. Faith links us savingly to Jesus, but inasmuch as it involves an acknowledgment that we have no merit of our own, it is confessedly not a meritorious work.

The gospel assures us that all who have entrusted their lives to Jesus Christ are born-again children of God (Jn. 1:12), indwelt, empowered, and assured of their status and hope by the Holy Spirit (Rom. 7:6, 8:9-17). The moment we truly believe in Christ, the Father declares us righteous in Him and begins conforming us to His likeness. Genuine faith acknowledges and depends upon Jesus as Lord and shows itself in growing obedience to the divine commands, though this contributes nothing to the ground of our justification (Jas. 2:14-26; Heb. 6:1-12).

By His sanctifying grace Christ works within us through faith, renewing our fallen nature and leading us to real maturity—that measure of development which is meant by "the fullness of Christ" (Eph. 4:13). The gospel calls us to live as obedient servants of Christ and as His emissaries in the world, doing justice, loving mercy, and helping all in need, thus seeking to bear witness to the kingdom of Christ. At death Christ takes the believer to Himself (Phil. 1:21) for unimaginable joy in the ceaseless worship of God (Rev. 22:1-5).

Salvation in its full sense is from the guilt of sin in the past, the power of sin in the present, and the presence of sin in the future. Thus, while in foretaste believers enjoy salvation now, they still await its fullness (Mk. 14: 61-62; Heb. 9:28). Salvation is a trinitarian reality, initiated by the Father, implemented by the Son, and applied by the Holy Spirit. It has a global dimension, for God's plan is to save believers out of every tribe and tongue (Rev. 5:9) to be His church, a new humanity, the people of God, the body and bride of Christ, and the community of the Holy Spirit. All the heirs of final salvation are called here and now to serve their Lord and each other in love, to share in the fellowship of Jesus' sufferings, and to work together to make Christ known to the whole world.

We learn from the gospel that as all have sinned, so all who do not receive Christ will be judged according to their just deserts as measured by God's holy law, and face eternal retributive punishment.

Unity in the Gospel

Christians are commanded to love each other despite differences of race, gender, privilege, and social, political, and economic background (Jn. 13:34-35; Gal. 3:28-29), and to be of one mind wherever possible (Jn. 17:20-21; Phil. 2:2; Rom. 14:1-15:13). We know that divisions among Christians hinder our witness in the world, and we desire greater mutual understanding and truth-speaking in love. We know too that as trustees of God's revealed truth we cannot embrace any form of doctrinal indifferentism, or relativism, or pluralism by which God's truth is sacrificed for a false peace.

Doctrinal disagreements call for debate. Dialogue for mutual understanding and, if possible, narrowing of the differences is valuable, doubly so when the avowed goal is unity in primary things, with liberty in secondary things, and charity in all things.

In the foregoing paragraphs an attempt has been made to state what is primary and essential in the gospel as evangelicals understand it. Useful dialogue, however, requires not only charity in our attitudes, but also clarity in our utterances. Our extended analysis of justification by faith alone through Christ alone reflects our belief that gospel truth is of crucial importance and is not always well understood and correctly affirmed. For added clarity, out of love for God's truth and Christ's church, we now cast the key points of what has been said into specific affirmations and denials regarding the gospel and our unity in it and in Christ.

Affirmations & Denials

1. **We affirm** that the gospel entrusted to the church is, in the first instance, God's gospel (Mk. 1:14; Rom. 1:1). God is its author and He reveals it to us in and by His Word. Its authority and truth rest on Him alone.

    We deny that the truth or authority of the gospel derives from any human insight or invention (Gal. 1:1-11). We also deny that the truth or authority of the gospel rests on the authority of any particular church or human institution.

2. **We affirm** that the gospel is the saving power of God in that the

gospel effects salvation to everyone who believes, without distinction (Rom. 1:16). This efficacy of the gospel is by the power of God Himself (1 Cor. 1:18).

We deny that the power of the gospel rests in the eloquence of the preacher, the technique of the evangelist, or the persuasion of rational argument (1 Cor. 1:21; 2:1-5).

3. **We affirm** that the gospel diagnoses the universal human condition as one of sinful rebellion against God, which if unchanged will lead each person to eternal loss under God's condemnation.

   We deny any rejection of the fallenness of human nature or any assertion of the natural goodness, or divinity, of the human race.

4. **We affirm** that Jesus Christ is the only way of salvation, the only mediator between God and humanity (Jn. 14:6; 1 Tim. 2:5).

   We deny that anyone is saved in any other way than by Jesus Christ and His gospel. The Bible offers no hope that sincere worshipers of other religions will be saved without personal faith in Jesus Christ.

5. **We affirm** that the church is commanded by God and is therefore under divine obligation to preach the gospel to every living person (Lk. 24:47; Mt. 28:18-19).

   We deny that any particular class or group of persons, whatever their ethnic or cultural identity, may be ignored or passed over in the preaching of the gospel (1 Cor. 9:19-22). God purposes a global church made up from people of every tribe, language, and nation (Rev. 7:9).

6. **We affirm** that faith in Jesus Christ as the divine Word or *Logos*, (Jn. 1:1), the second Person of the Trinity, co-eternal and co-essential with the Father and the Holy Spirit (Heb. 1:3), is foundational to faith in the gospel.

   We deny that any view of Jesus Christ which reduces or rejects His full deity is gospel faith or will avail to salvation.

7. **We affirm** that Jesus Christ is God incarnate (Jn. 1:14). The virgin-born descendant of David (Rom. 1:3), He had a true human nature, was subject to the Law of God (Gal. 4:5), and was like us

at all points, except without sin (Heb. 2:17, 7:26-28). **We affirm** that faith in the true humanity of Christ is essential to faith in the gospel.

We deny that anyone who rejects the humanity of Christ, His incarnation, or His sinlessness, or who maintains that these truths are not essential to the gospel, will be saved (1 Jn. 4:2-3).

8. **We affirm** that the atonement of Christ by which, in His obedience, He offered a perfect sacrifice, propitiating the Father by paying for our sins and satisfying divine justice on our behalf according to God's eternal plan, is an essential element of the gospel.

   We deny that any view of the atonement that rejects the substitutionary satisfaction of divine justice, accomplished vicariously for believers, is compatible with the teaching of the gospel.

9. **We affirm** that Christ's saving work included both His life and His death on our behalf (Gal. 3:13). We declare that faith in the perfect obedience of Christ by which He fulfilled all the demands of the Law of God in our behalf is essential to the gospel.

   We deny that our salvation was achieved merely or exclusively by the death of Christ without reference to His life of perfect righteousness.

10. **We affirm** that the bodily resurrection of Christ from the dead is essential to the biblical gospel (1 Cor. 15:14).

    We deny the validity of any so-called gospel that denies the historical reality of the bodily resurrection of Christ.

11. **We affirm** that the biblical doctrine of justification by faith alone in Christ alone is essential to the gospel (Rom. 3:28, 4:5; Gal. 2:16).

    We deny that any person can believe the biblical gospel and at the same time reject the apostolic teaching of justification by faith alone in Christ alone. We also deny that there is more than one true gospel (Gal. 1:6-9).

12. **We affirm** that the doctrine of the imputation (reckoning or counting) both of our sins to Christ and of His righteousness to us, whereby our sins are fully forgiven and we are fully accepted, is essential to the biblical gospel (2 Cor. 5:19-21).

We deny that we are justified by the righteousness of Christ infused into us or by any righteousness that is thought to inhere within us.

13. We affirm that the righteousness of Christ by which we are justified is properly His own, which He achieved apart from us, in and by His perfect obedience. This righteousness is counted, reckoned, or imputed to us by the forensic (that is, legal) declaration of God, as the sole ground of our justification.

    We deny that any works we perform at any stage of our existence add to the merit of Christ or earn for us any merit that contributes in any way to the ground of our justification (Gal. 2:16; Eph. 2:8,9; Titus 3:5).

14. We affirm that while all believers are indwelt by the Holy Spirit and are in the process of being made holy and conformed to the image of Christ, those consequences of justification are not its ground. God declares us just, remits our sins, and adopts us as His children, by His grace alone, and through faith alone, because of Christ alone, while we are still sinners (Rom. 4:5).

    We deny that believers must be inherently righteous by virtue of their cooperation with God's life-transforming grace before God will declare them justified in Christ. We are justified while we are still sinners.

15. We affirm that saving faith results in sanctification, the transformation of life in growing conformity to Christ through the power of the Holy Spirit. Sanctification means ongoing repentance, a life of turning from sin to serve Jesus Christ in grateful reliance on Him as one's Lord and Master (Gal. 5:22-25; Rom. 8:4,13-14).

    We reject any view of justification which divorces it from our sanctifying union with Christ and our increasing conformity to His image through prayer, repentance, cross-bearing, and life in the Spirit.

16. We affirm that saving faith includes mental assent to the content of the gospel, acknowledgment of our own sin and need, and personal trust and reliance upon Christ and His work.

    We deny that saving faith includes only mental acceptance of the gospel, and that justification is secured by a mere outward profession of faith. We further deny that any element of saving faith is a meritorious work or earns salvation for us.

17. We affirm that although true doctrine is vital for spiritual health and well-being, we are not saved by doctrine. Doctrine is necessary to inform us how we may be saved by Christ, but it is Christ who saves.

    We deny that the doctrines of the gospel can be rejected without harm. Denial of the gospel brings spiritual ruin and exposes us to God's judgment.

18. We affirm that Jesus Christ commands His followers to proclaim the gospel to all living persons, evangelizing everyone everywhere, and discipling believers within the fellowship of the church. A full and faithful witness to Christ includes the witness of personal testimony, godly living, and acts of mercy and charity to our neighbor, without which the preaching of the gospel appears barren.

    We deny that the witness of personal testimony, godly living, and acts of mercy and charity to our neighbors constitute evangelism apart from the proclamation of the gospel.

Our Commitment

As Evangelicals united in the gospel, we promise to watch over and care for one another, to pray for and forgive one another, and to reach out in love and truth to God's people everywhere, for we are one family, one in the Holy Spirit, and one in Christ.

Centuries ago it was truly said that in things necessary there must be unity, in things less than necessary there must be liberty, and in all things there must be charity. We see all these gospel truths as necessary.

Now to God, the Author of the truth and grace of this gospel, through Jesus Christ, its subject and our Lord, be praise and glory for ever and ever.

Amen.

© Copyright 1999 by
The Committee on Evangelical Unity in the Gospel
Post Office Box 5551, Glendale Heights, IL 60139-5551

Declaration of Intent

IN THE NAME OF THE LORD JESUS CHRIST, the central focus in every God-given corporate revival . . .

With the growing conviction that a general moral and spiritual awakening to Christ is the desperate need of our churches and of our nation as a whole . . .

Out of an increasing sense of urgency for Christian leaders and churches in America to find new levels of consensus and collaboration concerning the biblical nature and hope of corporate revival . . .

With personal determination to no longer simply be for corporate revival, but rather to be wholeheartedly about the work of appealing to both God and to my fellow believers for corporate revival . . .

And realizing my own perpetual need for a fresh work of Christ in personal revival even as I seek corporate revival . . .

WITH GREAT HOPE IN GOD, I solemnly join with other churches and leaders across America in this Declaration of Intent . . .

- I will PERCEIVE . . . Because God has awakened me to the urgent need and multitude of biblical promises for Christ-centered revival among Christians and churches, I will continue building my vision for this through Scripture, study, prayer, and interaction with believers similarly awakened. *And I will appeal to others to do the same.*
- I will PRIORITIZE . . . Out of my commitment to the supremacy of Christ in His church, I will reorder my walk with Him and my ministry for Him, so that I am found to be constantly living for corporate revival in my church, and in our nation. *And I will appeal to others to do the same.*
- I will PURIFY . . . Because corporate revival is an extraordinary work of the Holy Spirit, I will repent as a way of life, confessing and turning from everything that grieves, quenches, resists, or disobeys the ministry of the Spirit. *And I will appeal to others to do the same.*

- I will PRAY . . . In concert with the groundswell of prayer for awakening and revival across the body of Christ in this generation, I will intercede (both alone and with others) for corporate revival as a key dimension of my daily walk with Christ. *And I will appeal to others to do the same.*
- I will PROCLAIM . . . Since biblical revival must be anchored in God's Word, and because faith for corporate revival comes by hearing the promises and discovering the ways of God in revival, I will let this message of repentance and hope dominate my conversations with and ministry to Christians and churches where God places me. *And I will appeal to others to do the same.*
- I will PREPARE . . . Since I expect God to ultimately answer our prayers, fulfill His promises, and grant corporate revival to Christians and churches in America, I will start living now, in all areas of discipleship and church activity, in anticipation of and full readiness for the spiritual awakening to Christ for which we wait. *And I will appeal to others to do the same.*
- I will PARTNER . . . Because the hope of impending corporate revival requires a new era of consensus and collaboration among leaders and churches in America, I will be proactive in encouraging associations, networks, and coalitions (especially at the local community level) among believers committed to the hope of a spiritual awakening to Christ. *And I will appeal to others to do the same.*

To join your name with others who are committing themselves to be about revival, please fill out the commitment card at the back of this booklet and send it to:

An Urgent Appeal
c/o Harvest Prayer Ministries
455 Springhill Drive
Terre Haute, IN 47802

Or go to www.urgentappeal.net to register your intent. You will also find more information on the Urgent Appeal at this website.

Teaching Curriculum for Urgent Appeal Facilitators

This outline accompanies a training video prepared by the National Revival Network, America's National Prayer Committee, and Mission America—co-sponsors of *An Urgent Appeal* document and the Urgent Appeal Campaign. At the request of the three coalitions, the outline was developed by David Bryant, based on his experience in conducting 10 Living Room Events, in different regions and with a variety of ethnic and denominational leadership participating. The suggested guidelines can equip any facilitator to lead similar events in his or her own community.

A "Living Room Event" can take anywhere from two-and-a-half to four hours, depending on your audience and the context. The outline below can be collapsed or expanded in time, primarily based on how "group interaction exercises" are conducted. Watch the training video keeping this curriculum close by so you can see how to best facilitate a discussion of *An Urgent Appeal* booklet. Beside the facilitator having this booklet, it is highly recommended that each participant has a copy.

Outline

Session I
- Get acquainted
- Introduction to the reason we're here
- What is the Spirit saying to the churches today?
- A glance at the document
- So . . . What do we think about "revival"/"corporate revival"?
- When we come back
- Closing prayer time

Break

Session II
- Background on the Campaign
- Overall vision for the Campaign
- A walk through the document
- Open discussion by the group
- Next steps after today
- Conclusion of Living Room Event (Praying through the Urgent Appeal)

Session I

GET AQUAINTED
Go around the room and tell three things about yourself: name, church, a Bible character you are most like and why (one sentence only).

INTRODUCTION TO THE REASON WE'RE HERE
- Opening story or two ("Taxi Driver"/"Presbyterian on Revival").
- We are here to explore two major themes: Urgency/Revival.
- Is there an urgency for a new work of God in the church? Is that to be a work of corporate revival?
- We are here to explore two major responses: Consensus/Collaboration.
- Is there a way to reach consensus on the topic of revival? If so, are there ways that leaders can collaborate for that God-given work? If so, is it urgent that this happen? And, can it happen here?

WHAT IS THE SPIRIT SAYING TO THE CHURCHES TODAY?
- Story: Billy Graham on Larry King; "Mel Blanc-Which voice is yours?"
- September 11: Wake up call; refocus priorities; listen for a word from heaven.
- Revelation 2-3: In times of crisis the Spirit desires to speak, for us to hear
- What do *you* think the Spirit's agenda is for the church right now? Large group brainstorming. Possible answers: judgment, reconciliation, unity, focus on Israel, moral crisis, call to holiness, focus on Islam, etc.
- George Barna's perspective (based on year-long research in 2000):

    "The nation seems mired in spiritual complacency. America certainly did not experience the spiritual revival that many Christians hoped would emerge as the new millennium began. In fact, Americans seemed to have become inoculated to spiritual events, outreach efforts, and the quest for personal spiritual development.

    "Overall, Christian ministry is stuck in a deep rut. Our research continues to point out the need for more urgent reliance upon God to change people's lives. Too many Christians and churches in America have traded in spiritual passion for empty rituals, clever methods, and mindless practices.

    "The challenge to today's church is not methodological. It

is the challenge to resuscitate the spiritual passion and fervor of the nation's Christians."
- Barna adds research on 66 moral categories; on 40% pastors ready to quit.
- What do *you* think about Barna's sense of the Spirit's agenda for the church?

(Open discussion)

- OVERVIEW of what recent surveys seems to suggest. There are at least seven major concerns many leaders are identifying. This became quite evident working on the document *An Urgent Appeal*:
  1) Our generation is at a crossroads with God
  2) Our nation is in crisis
  3) The church is in crisis
  4) Our only lasting hope is Divine intervention ("revival")
  5) There are some wonderful signs of hope that God is at work
  6) We must act now to seek consensus and collaboration to that end
  7) Christ must be kept at the center of God's intervention

A GLANCE AT THE DOCUMENT
- Look at the title . . . consider each word and its importance (see pages 8-9)

HOW THE DOCUMENT CAME INTO BEING
- Sponsors: National Revival Network (NRN) . . . then America's National Prayer Committee (NPC) and Mission America (MA)
- Six major drafts . . . more than 100 national Christian leaders . . . very diverse
- Well-received (response of a Ph.D church history prof)
- Not intended to be a "primer" on revival
- Rather, this is a "conversation starter" . . . based on the assumption that most leaders already have done some solid thinking on the biblical theme of revival
- A tool to explore if consensus and collaboration are possible and urgent
- Let's read the objectives (see page 7)
- There has never been anything like this before.
- Designed to preempt the problems of previous Great Awakenings and help us to be ready for a fresh work of God

SO . . . WHAT DO WE THINK ABOUT "REVIVAL"/"CORPORATE REVIVAL"?

- Story on revival (New York City: Epicenter of three Great Awakenings)
- Private Reflection: Take a sheet of paper. Write down the following:
    One word definition for revival (Ill: "resuscitate")
    Think of a "picture" (metaphor) for revival (use in a slide show)
    One short biblical passage that touches on revival
    Share one word around the room; then have them look at p. 17
    Share passage in groups of three
- Slide show: (Click) "What do you see?" (Share one by one)

CONSIDER ISAIAH . . .
- 44 — outpouring; think flowers in a desert
- 52:1-3; 60:1-3 — awakening; think waking up this morning
- 64:1-4 — rending heavens; think curtain at a play

BIBLICAL OVERVIEW:
- OT — Prototypes: The Exodus; Judges; 2 Chronicles; Haggai
- NT — Case Studies: Acts; Prayers of Paul; 2 Thess. 3:1; Mk. 1:15
- Church History — Dr. Ebenezer Porter (1830-eyewitness):

> "The history of these revivals shows that the genuine tendency of such seasons is to render Christians grateful, watchful, fervent in spirit. Many, doubtless, must be viewed as sincere Christians who are not consistent Christians. The wise and foolish virgins slumber together, while the bridegroom tarries. But when the Redeemer comes in the triumphs of His grace to visit His churches, then His true followers are seen waking from their apathy, and going forth to welcome the King of Zion with an energy and earnestness and ardor of affection greatly surpassing their first love."

LECTURES ON REVIVAL
- How do you respond to Porter's definition of corporate revival?

(Brief open discussion)

WHEN IT TOUCHED ME: (Kent State; 2 Corinthians 1 at a crisis moment in ministry)

SIGNS IN OUR GENERATION: prayer movements; coalitions; renewal movements; youth awakenings; in other nations

IT IS A GROWING HOPE: more frequently mentioned; conferences on it; books on it; focus of millions of prayers; solid reason (see page 24)
- Small group discussion: "Do *you* see any reasons for hope? If so, what are they? If not, why is that?"

GREAT NEED OF THE HOUR: "Start the conversation—now!" The purpose of the Urgent Appeal Campaign is to do this very thing.

WHEN WE COME BACK . . .
- Background on the Campaign
- What the campaign ultimately envisions
- Role of the document to "Start the conversation-now!"
- Overview of the document
- Open preliminary discussion of the issues
- Extended prayer
- Possibilities and steps from here

CLOSING PRAYER TIME: What do you most need to say to the Father right now? (Small groups)

Break for Refreshments

Session Ii

Opening Story: (Stamp: United We Stand/ National Day of Prayer: America United Under God)

BACKGROUND ON THE CAMPAIGN
- "Urgent Appeals" in Scripture: Hezekiah (read 2 Chron. 30:5-12); Habakkuk 2; Haggai; Invitation for banquet (Luke 14); Words of Paul in 2 Corinthians 5 (persuade, appeal, beg)
- The vision for "urgent appeals" in previous revivals. (Another word from Porter lectures:)

"I would by all means advise you to avoid that hesitating and paralyzing apprehension which leads a minister to be so much afraid of being wrong as to do nothing. Under God, the ministers of the 19th century [or, 21st century] have a mighty work to accomplish. Our own vast country is to be brought under the influence of the Gospel. The wide world is to be evangelized. The day of slumber is passed. The sacramental host of God's elect is marshaled in arms, and wait for ministers to lead them on to victory. Gird on your armor, then, soldiers of the cross! The Captain of salvation heads the van, having on His vesture and on His thigh a name written: King of Kings and Lord of Lords! He has gone forth in the triumphs of His grace, conquering and to conquer. Stubborn hearts, in numbers unexampled, bow before the all-subduing influences of His Spirit." (Lectures on Revival)

HOW DID THIS \CAMPAIGN EVOLVE:
- Nationwide Call to Prayer from Mission America in *USA TODAY*, etc.
- Meeting of NRN: in prayer came the word "urgent"
- Development of the document . . . "to start the conversation now"
- Presented to Mission America . . . another year of input from scores of leaders
- Adopted by National Prayer Committee as a major "project" in May 2001
- Presented to 5,000 pastors in Orlando, January 2002
- Presented via "Nationally Broadcast Concert of Prayer" to whole hemisphere
- Development of "Spanish" and "Youth" versions
- Development of a potent website (www.urgentappeal.net)
- Field tests of "Living Room Events," interfacing with NPC/MA field staff
- Video-training tool developed to rapidly multiply Living Room Events
- Training of national leaders in D.C. following National Day of Prayer activities, May 2002
- Why word "CAMPAIGN"? . . . Consider a "political campaign"; due to sense of urgency

OVERALL VISION FOR THE CAMPAIGN
- Thousands of Living Room Events, sponsored and facilitated by local leadership
- Pastor "Conversation Cells" form, to spend next six weeks working through questions for six sections of document; lay people also form cells
- Conclude six weeks by determining response to: Declaration of Intent
- Beyond Declaration, determine together: If there's consensus, how can we collaborate?
- Goal: Pastors (and lay leaders) laboring together for corporate revival where they live.
- Goal: Theme of biblical revival becomes a dominant theme at all levels of ministry.
- Goal: To flood the church with "Messengers of Hope" at every level.

WHAT IS THE ROLE OF THE DOCUMENT?
- Not a primer on revival, but it does synthesize and bring under one cover many of the most critical themes for exploring (conversing on) corporate revival.
- Arranges major themes in a logical flow of topics for

maximum effectiveness. The "conversation" moves through six major sections.
- Saves busy leaders the need to do a lot of initial research (document represents literally hundreds of hours of research by NRN "drafting committee" and others)
- Designed to get the conversation started, and to help leaders identify what they already believe about the issues—corporate revival, urgency, collaboration, etc.

A WALK THROUGH THE DOCUMENT
Simply walk through it, turning the pages, stopping to highlight a thought here or there, such as:
- p. 5—call to prayer
- p. 9—six bullets on what document will do
- p. 9—desire to make it personal and how this can be done
- p. 14—sample of questions for conversation
- p. 15—only place scholars are quoted, and why its done here
- p. 19—insuring that all conversations on revival are Christo-centric
- p. 23—why the need for an "apologetic" and the value of having it
- p. 27—clarifications: three key ones here, plus a set of questions in the Appendix. Again, this is simply designed to get a conversation started.
- p. 31—series of cautions: nothing like this was ever confronted before previous revivals. What a difference it makes to face them in a pre-revival time.
- p. 35—seven "Ps" summarize most of what all the great literature on revival suggests we need to do to be ready. Here are ways to collaborate. Reflected in the "Declaration of Intent" (see page 55).

Also, take a moment to explain why the document "Evangelical Celebration of the Gospel" was included in a document on corporate revival (pages 45-53).

OPEN DISCUSSION BY THE GROUP (Take questions in any order)
- What do you like about the document? How might it be helpful?
- What questions does the approach of the document raise for you?
- What currently hinders consensus among us on corporate revival? What are the biggest conceptual obstacles?
- What currently hinders collaboration among us on corporate revival? What are the biggest practical/logistical obstacles?

- What steps might we take together to overcome obstacles to consensus? Or, to collaboration? Could this document—and the six weekly studies—be useful?
- Does the whole issue of corporate revival—local or national—have a ring of urgency for you? Why or why not?
- Does the concept of being "about" revival, not just "for" revival, make sense to you? If so, which are you and why?
- How do you react to the "Declaration of Intent" overall? How do you respond to the issues it outlines?
- Would you be interested in joining a "Conversation Cell" for the next six weeks? How do you see that coming together for you?

NEXT STEPS AFTER TODAY
- Consider signing the Declaration of Intent (read it out loud in unison)
- Spend a season of prayer right now, addressing some of the vision and concerns that have surfaced throughout the Living Room Event. Depending on the quality of discussions, and the time left for prayer, you might consider using the document: "Praying Through the Urgent Appeal" (Available at www.urgentappeal.net.) The same outline might be used for an in-depth prayer time following the six weeks of "Conversation Cells", when participants reconvene as a whole to discuss next steps in collaboration.
- Decide *who* wants to begin a "Conversation Cell" and *how* it will happen.

CONCLUSION OF THE LIVING ROOM EVENT
- The "urgent appeal" is really in *three* directions: (1) God's appeal to us . . . (2) Our appeal to God . . . (3) Our appeal to each other and to the people we serve.
- Closing story (Yonggi Cho on Mt.. 11:12)

"Let the conversation begin . . . now!"
"And let it begin with me."